W9-BVQ-553

Table of Contents

Author

Barbara Bateman, Ph.D., J.D., began her special education career in the 1950s in public schools and institutions where she taught children who had mental retardation, visual impairments, autism, speech and language disorders, dyslexia and other disabilities. She conducted research on learning disabilities with Dr. Samuel Kirk at the University of Illinois. In 1966 she returned to Oregon and since then has taught special education and special education law at the University of Oregon. In 1976 she graduated from the University of Oregon School of Law. Presently, Dr. Bateman is a consultant in special education law. She consults with and provides training to parents, attorneys, school districts and others involved in special education legal disputes. Her publications number over 100 and include Writing Measurable IEP Goals and Objectives (2006), Why Johnny Doesn't Behave: Twenty Tips for Measurable BIPS (2003) and Better IEP Meetings (2006), a companion volume to Better IEPs (2006).

Dr. Bateman's current professional priorities include writing, conducting professional training in IEP development, evaluating IEPs, assessing program appropriateness for individual students, presenting IDEA to parents and school personnel and serving as an expert witness in special education cases. Less professional interests include travel and birding, in the largest possible doses.

Introduction to Gobbledygooks

No one is born knowing how to drive a car or send an email. Some skills have to be learned. One of these is writing measurable goals. When we find goal writing difficult and frustrating, as so many do, it is because we haven't been taught how to write goals easily and well. The good news is that writing measurable goals really isn't hard, once the mystery is taken away and the steps revealed.

The purpose of this down-to-earth, plain English guide is to do just that — to strip away the mystique and demonstrate how to move our first, often foggy thoughts about a possible goal — we call that a Gobbledygook (GG) — to a clean, objective and truly measurable goal. Real IEPs are full of Gobbledygooks and for this book we have taken some — every one from an actual child's IEP — and shown exactly how to convert each to a useful and measurable goal.

In converting each Gobbledygook (GG) to a useful, measurable goal we have tried to determine what the writer of the GG was trying to say, i.e., to be true to the intent of the original non-measurable goal. Some conversions are very simple, e.g., "Tim will cross the street safely 80% of the time," becomes Tim will cross the street safely 100% of the time." Others are more difficult. We found one that totally defies translation — "Tyler will navigate the world in school." Who could possibly know what the writer of that GG had in mind?

In the discussion that follows each GG we "think aloud" the actual process of fixing that particular GG. We have shared drafts of this material with real teachers who have to write IEP goals and who, like the writers of our GGs, have not had adequate instruction in writing measurable objective goals. Several teachers expressed difficulty in grasping why the commonly used "80% of the time" criterion is not measurable and how "80% of the time" is different from "80% (or 4 of

5) of the times" or "opportunities" a task is attempted. Another source of difficulty is "80% accuracy" in tasks such as initiating conversation. How would one determine whether a conversation was initiated with 80% accuracy? (In the discussions we deal with these and other common problems.) As we move in the following pages from each GG to the discussion and then to a real and measurable goal, we must always keep in mind the question "**How** can one determine whether the goal has been reached?" How can we **measure** the student's performance? A well written goal makes very clear exactly how it can be measured. Each measurable goal below is followed by the "how" of determining (i.e., measuring) whether it has or has not been reached:

> **Goal:** Weigh no more than 130 pounds on June 1.
> **Measurement:** On June 1, step on a scale.

> **Goal:** Read 110 "Easy Sight Words" orally in one minute with no more than two errors by June 1.
> **Measurement:** Ask child to read aloud the 110 word list. Time him and count the errors, if any.

> **Goal:** Interact appropriately with at least one peer for a total of 5 minutes during morning recess, for two consecutive days.
> **Measurement:** Observe and time the duration of the child's interactions during recess for two consecutive days.

The next examples are Gobbledygooks precisely because it isn't clear how one could determine (measure) whether the goal had been reached:

> **GG:** Be respectful 90% of the time.
> **Measurement:** ?

"If a goal is explicit and transparent, how to assess whether it has been reached should be evident in the goal itself."

GG: Take more responsibility for her behavior.
Measurement: ?

GG: Maintain one friendship with 80% accuracy.
Measurement: ?

After the discussion of each GG, explaining why it isn't acceptable, our new measurable goal is presented. Finally, for each measurable goal, a "test" is briefly presented in which we check to be sure the new goal contains the required elements of measurability — an observable behavior and an objective criterion.

Measurable goals are measurable goals, whether we talk about saving a certain dollar amount for our retirement nest egg, manufacturing a certain number of widgets per week, or orally reading so many words per minute correct from a third grade reader. All measurable goals must have an **observable behavior** (e.g., saving dollars, manufacturing widgets or orally reading words) and an **objective criterion** (e.g., 600 widgets per week or 80 words correct per minute). Some measurable goals also require a given or a condition, e.g., "given a third grade reader," or "given access to the internet." Often the given is implicit in the goal. With a street crossing goal it is not necessary to say "given a street . . ."

As just said, all measurable goals have observable behavior and an objective criterion stating the desired level of performance — how much must be done or how well it must be done to meet the goal. Some goals must also specify the condition under which the behavior is to be done.

Proper goals refer only to students' behavior (not that of teachers) and do not include instructions as a given because instruction is always assumed. Goals like "gains in height," which ordinarily require the passage of time rather than instruction, are also not appropriate for IEP goals. Whether the means of measurement should be included in an IEP goal is another related issue. If a goal is sufficiently explicit and transparent, the method of assessing whether it has been reached is almost always evident in the goal itself.

Every measurable goal (a) allows a clear yes or no determination as to whether it has been reached; (b) can be reliably assessed, i.e., different evaluators can agree on whether it was accomplished; (c) requires no additional information for assessment, unlike a goal of "improving X" which requires further explanation about the beginning point; and (d) tells the evaluators exactly what to do to determine whether the goal was reached, such as counting the widgets or measuring how high the bar is placed for the high jumpers. Measurable goals have these characteristics because they contain observable behaviors and definite objective criteria.

In addition to these basic features of all measurable goals, IEP measurable annual goals must have other characteristics in order to be useful and to comply with the Individuals with Disabilities Education Act (IDEA). IEP annual goals must also:

1. Address all the student's unique educational needs;

2. Project an amount of progress over the year which assumes intensive appropriate instruction and takes into account the child's ability level;

3. Reflect the important, high priority skills or knowledge for the student at this point in time, as determined by parents, teachers and others who know the child and his or her needs; and

4. Be grounded in explicit, detailed and completely current **present levels of performance** (PLOPs). For example, if the goal is to "read

orally fourth grade materials at 110 correct words per minute," the PLOP must be in the IEP in the same terms, e.g., now "reads third grade material at 60 correct words per minute." (Many examples will be provided later — for now the rule is that a measurable goal must have a corresponding measured present level of performance in the IEP.)

The Importance of Measurable Annual IEP Goals

Since IDEA was revised in 2004, measurable annual goals are more important than ever. Two of the purposes of IDEA 2004 are to "improve educational results" and "to assess and ensure the effectiveness of education for children who have disabilities." In the IDEA 2004 findings Congress declared that "Improving education results for children with disabilities is an essential element of our national policy ..."

While emphasizing results and effectiveness (reaching goals) of special education, Congress paradoxically deleted, for two thirds of the special education students, the important requirement that each goal have measurable short term objectives (or benchmarks). The mandatory short term objectives remain only for those students who are assessed using alternate (i.e., not grade level) standards. Best practice, of course, still demands the use of short term objectives, and IDEA still requires that the child's progress be meaningfully reported to parents at least every grading period. Without objective, measurable and measured objectives, benchmarks or other progress markers, one cannot fulfill this requirement to inform parents about the effectiveness of their child's special education program. Thus both best practice and mandated progress measurement argue for continuing the use of short objectives, at least one per grading period.

Some wise states and school districts are voluntarily continuing this best practice and are using short term objectives as the required IEP progress markers. Others are not. Either way, the reality is that more attention than ever will now be focused on the MEASURABLE ANNUAL GOALS and whether they are written in such a way that progress toward them can be and is objectively assessed and meaningfully reported to parents. State monitors, hearing officers, administrative law judges, and courts will surely scrutinize goals for measurability far more closely than ever before since all of IDEA's mandated progress reporting "eggs" are now in the "goals basket."

Let us recall that a measurable goal is on the IEP to be **measured**. More attention will inevitably be focused on when and how progress toward the goal was assessed.

Recent court and due process hearing decisions show this increased attention to measurability and measuring. In looking at the following quotations from cases, remember that an inappropriate IEP usually constitutes a denial of a free appropriate public education (FAPE), and that a denial of FAPE can lead to very serious financial consequences for the district.

Goals Must Allow Progress Assessment and Progress Must Be Assessed

An Alabama decision emphasized the importance of measurability of goals for progress assessment:

(Measurable goals) must provide a mechanism for determining whether the placement and services are enabling the child to make educational progress. Annual goals or statements should describe what the child can reasonably be expected to accomplish during the year in the special education program ...

Periodic review of progress on the goals and objectives provides the disabled student's teacher with supportive data needed to make a determination of the success of the intervention and strategies employed. (*Escambia Co. Public Sch. System*, 42 IDELR 248 (SEA AL 2004)).

A hearing decision which superbly illustrates one hearing officer's mastery of relevant law and her thorough understanding of special education addressed two all too common inappropriate IEP reading goals. The first goal says that, "Student will increase his reading comprehension skills by improving his decoding skills with 80% of accuracy." A later goal is identical except the accuracy was now 85%. The hearing officer appropriately found that:

These statements of annual goals and short-term objectives are not sufficient to satisfy the purpose of the measurable annual goals and objectives requirement. The purpose of measurable goals and objectives is to 'enable a child's teacher(s), parents and others involved in developing and implementing the child's IEP, to gauge, at intermediate times during the year, how well the child is progressing toward achievement of the annual goal.' ... This information allows the IEP team to determine whether a child is making adequate progress, and, if not, to revise the IEP accordingly ... The United States Department of Education describes measurable goals and short-term objectives as 'critical to the strategic planning used to develop and implement the IEP for each child with disability.' (Internal citations omitted)[1] (*Rio Rancho Public Schools*, 40 IDELR 140 (SEA NM 2003))

A New York hearing officer succinctly noted:

[B]oth the 2000-01 IEP and 2001-02 IEP were deficient in that they lacked adequate objective data by which to measure the student's present levels of performance in reading and language arts. The lack of objective data resulted in an inadequate basis upon which to measure his progress in those areas and to develop meaningful, measurable goals and objectives. (*Bd. of Ed. of the Rhinebeck Central Sch. Dist.*, 39 IDELR 148 (SEA NY 2003))

About the common practice of using teacher observation to assess progress, the same hearing officer observed this:

Although subjective teacher observation provides valuable information, teacher observation by itself, is not an adequate method of monitoring a student's progress in his areas of academic needs, particularly when a baseline has not been established. Moreover, the record reveals that the student's teacher was not certain of the student's levels of functioning or how well he progressed from year to year. I, therefore, find that the 2000-01 IEP failed to set forth adequately measurable goals and objectives. (*id*)

---

[1]Internal (within the quotation) legal citations are omitted from the quotes for ease of reading.

Goals Must Objectively Specify the Level of Achievement to Be Reached

The excellent New Mexico hearing officer quoted earlier has explained that:

> A goal of "increasing reading comprehension skills" or "improving decoding skills" is not a measurable goal without a clear statement of Student's present level of performance and a specific objective against which Student's progress can be measured. Even if present level of performance were clearly stated, an open-ended statement that Student will "improve" does not meet the requirement (added by the 1997 amendments to the IDEA) for a "measurable" goal. The addition of a percentage of accuracy is not helpful where the IEP fails to define a starting point, an ending point, the curriculum in which Student will achieve 80 or 85% accuracy or a procedure for pre-and post-testing of Student. (*Rio Rancho Public Schools*, supra)

Another hearing officer stated it similarly:

> [T]hese goals and objectives, as written, are too vague and immeasurable to meet the requirement set forth in state and federal regulations. For example, all of the goals specify the student must "Demonstrate an improvement" but do not state how ... The writing goals states "Demonstrate an improvement in the mechanics of written language such as spelling, capitalization and punctuation necessary to write for information, understanding and written expression," but the expectation as to how the student will demonstrate the improvements in the areas listed in the goal is unknown. More specificity is required in an

IEP goal and/or objective. (*Bd. of Ed. of the Carmel Sch. Dist.* 43 IDELR 76 (SEA NY 2005)).

Two additional hearing officers were more succinct:

"Language in the IEP goals which specified P. 'would improve' was not designed to provide any indication of measurable achievement. (*Mobile Co. Bd. of Ed.*, 40 IDLER 226 (SEA AL 2004))," and "The goals do not appear to be measurable, missing a criterion to determine if they were reached . . . (*Lancaster Sch. Dist.*, 39 IDLER 118 (SEA PA 2003))"

Goals Must Address All of the Students Unique Educational Needs and Must Be Tightly Aligned to the Present Levels of Performance (PLOPs) in each area of need, and to the Services

Numerous cases have addressed the necessity of the IEP addressing all areas of the student's needs by having PLOPs, goals and services for each. A few excerpts illustrate this:

. . . The IEP failed to consider D.C.'s non-academic difficulties, which included depression and suicidal tendencies, as well as regular harassment and physical abuse by his schoolmate . . . (*Montgomery Township Bd. of Ed. v. S.C.*, 43 IDELR 186 (3rd Cir. 2005)) (unpublished case)

. . . [The IEP] did not contain measurable annual goals in written expression and spelling, fundamental areas in which the child experienced deficiencies. Given the evidence, we conclude . . . that the IEP was inadequate . . . (*Pawling Central Sch. Dist. v. N.Y. State Ed.* Dept., 40 IDLER 180 (N.Y. Supreme Court, App. Div. 2004))

When analyzed in light of Student's unique profile, however, the proposed program for 2004-2005 was not appropriate for Student at the time it was offered . . . because it did not adequately address Student's well-documented auditory processing and attention issue. The weight of the evidence shows that Student is simply too easily distracted and has too many problems with auditory processing and auditory memory to be able to function successfully in a setting where multiple activities are going on within earshot. (*North Reading Public Schools*, 43 IDELR 178 (SEA MA 2005))

Another decision on point states:

The Hearing Officer finds that addressing a student's identified needs by way of an informal program that is not guided by goals and objectives does not meet state and federal standards for the proper development of an IEP . . . It is true that a student is not entitled to a "Cadillac education"; however, both state and federal law require that the IEP contain measurable annual goals, including benchmarks or short-term objectives, related to the student's needs that result from the student's disability. The IEP . . . did not meet this standard because it did not contain goals and objectives designed to address STUDENT'S unique receptive and expressive language needs.

The Hearing Officer concludes that because the IEP did not include goals and objectives addressing receptive and expressive language deficits, the IEP was not designed to meet STUDENT'S unique needs and therefore, was not reasonably calculated to provide STUDENT with educational benefit. Accordingly, the IEP . . . was not an offer of a FAPE. (*Lancaster Sch. Dist.*, supra)

The essential and integral relationship among PLOPs, goals, and services is unequivocally stated in a California case:

"The IEP must also show a direct relationship between the student present levels of educational performance, the goals, and services that are to be provided to meet these goals." (*Simi Valley Unified Sch. Dist.*, 44 IDLER 106 (SEA CA 2005))

The next case deals with a mismatch between PLOPs and goals and the difficulties presented by PLOPs and goals so vague one cannot ascertain the relationship between them:

> The 2001-2002 IEP lacked accurate measurable goals and appropriate strategies for evaluating the student's progress. It included goals that the student would increase his writing skills "to pass the eighth grade assessment" and that he would increase his reading comprehension skills to the 6.5 grade level.... However, his teacher testified that he was not close to being able to pass the eighth grade writing assessment and the neuropsychologist had reported in December 2000 that he was reading at only a third grade level and that his writing skills were at a first grade level. Again, the IEP did not include any updated testing in reading and writing to determine the efficacy of the program it provided. (*Bd. of Ed. of the Rhinebeck Central Sch. Dist.*, supra)

Finally the last case touches on many aspects of inadequate PLOPs and goals:

> The IHO found that the portions of the IEPs dedicated to describing Christopher's present levels of performance were

inadequate because the IEPs did not provide information "related to the Student's specific skills deficits in attention, organization, behavioral compliance and social interaction." The same goals and objectives were later repeated in the Student's fourth grade IEP. The IHO also found that the annual goal components of the IEP were "so vague they are immeasurable." The IHO came to this conclusion because a number of the terms set out could not be objectively evaluated.

The Court finds that the IEPs developed by the School District were inadequate as to the "present levels of performance" and "goals and objectives" sections. The "present levels of performance sections of Christopher's IEPs contain only conclusory statements about Christopher's present level of abilities and the IEPs do not fully explain how Christopher's disability affects his involvement in the educational process. For instance, the 2001-2002 IEP discusses only very generally Christopher's difficulties in interacting socially with other students.

In addition, the Court finds that the sections of Christopher's IEPs dedicated to "goals and objectives" are inadequate. Christopher's IEP for the 2000-2001 school year states only that: "[Student] will improve his behavior from non-appropriate to appropriate through teacher intervention and small group instruction by 10-01." This goal is repeated in Christopher's 2001-2002 IEP. The wording of the goal and the short-term objectives that follow is very vague and could define a broad range of conduct. The short-term objectives provide that the objectives will be met according to certain percentages, but the short term objectives do not provide objective criteria against which achievement can be measured. Based on an evaluation of Christopher's IEPs and the criteria against which Christopher's achievements are to be measured, the Court affirms the findings of the IHO and HRO and finds that the "present levels of performance" and "goals and objectives sections" of Christopher's IEPs were inadequate. (*Larson v. ISD # 361*, 40 IDLER 231 (D. MN 2004))

From Gobbledygooks to Measurable Goals

The GGs that follow are all taken from real IEPs, most written within the last three years. They embody a wide range of difficulties, all common but none more so than the misuse of percentage. Whoever started the erroneous belief that inserting a percentage (usually between 70% and 95%, most often 80% or 85%) into a goal makes it measurable has done the field of special education a huge disfavor. The GGs that follow are in no particular order. They are not organized by the type of error or the topic they illustrate. However, *Tables 1* and *2* (pages 20-21) provide the numbers of the GGs that (a) illustrate a particular error such as misuse of percentage, and (b) that deal with a topic such as reading or social skills.

Table

1

Types of Problems in Gobbledygooks

Type of Problem	Number of Gobbledygooks[2]
1. Wording is jargon or too vague, broad, or fuzzy	4, 6, 7, 8, 10, 13, 14, 18, 20, 23, 26, 28, 29, 30, 31
2. Misuse of percentage, such as 80% of the time	1, 2, 3, 5, 6, 9, 15, 23, 25, 30
3. Standards-based, not individualized	10, 11, 12, 13, 17, 35
4. Inadequate or absent performance criterion	2, 3, 16, 17, 19, 20, 21, 22, 26, 27
5. Goal does not align with PLOP or child's ability	11, 12, 24, 28, 32, 33
6. Absence of common sense	1, 8
7. Misuse of "given" or inappropriate	27, 34
8. No student behavior	28

[2]Many of the GG examples have more than one problem, so they appear more than once.

Topics of Gobbledygooks & Examples

Table 2

Topic	Number of Gobbledygooks
1. Self-help skills	1, 22
2. Social skills	2, 5, 7, 21, 28, 30
3. Language	15, 23, 25, 31, 32, 34
4. Academics	
a. Reading	8, 10, 24, 29, 33
b. Writing	18, 19, 27
c. Arithmetic	16, 20,
d. Telling time	9
e. Science, Health	11, 12, 13, 17
5. Classroom behavior; inappropriate behavior	3, 6, 14, 26
6. Fine motor skills	4
7. Defies classification; must see to believe	35

Each GG is followed by a discussion designed to show why the GG is just that — gobbledygook — and how the GG can be converted into a legally correct and useful measurable goal. An early step is to attempt to ascertain what goal the writer of the GG was attempting to formulate. That is not always possible, but we make a reasonable guess and then begin the process.

One of the many problems with the GGs is just that they do not always reveal what is intended. So, dear reader, it is very possible that when you read a GG, you might suppose the person who wrote it intended a real goal different from the one that is suggested. You may be absolutely right — which is exactly why each goal writer must learn to write clearly what she or he meant. Our hope and belief is that the examples that follow will enable one to move readily, precisely and confidently to do just that — to write goals easily, clearly and in measurable terms that tell what the child will be able to do when the time comes to assess progress.

The format in each illustrative GG will be:

(a) the GG as it appeared on the actual IEP;

(b) a discussion of what is wrong with the GG and thoughts on making it into a measurable goal;

(c) the measurable goal itself; and

(d) the test for measurability, i.e., checking to see if the goal contains an observable behavior and an objective criterion.

—Note—
On page 28 of the next chapter, an introductory Gobbledygook is given, then rendered into a measurable goal.

The assumption is that many of us begin our thought process about a goal with something close to GG and then try to improve it by adding "85%" or a similar gimmick we were erroneously taught to believe would make it measurable. On some of the GGs we provide basic information about the real child for whom it was written. This is necessary when, for example, the problem is a total mismatch among the child's PLOPs, ability level and the goal. The match between the child's PLOPs and the projected goal is both critical and too often overlooked. *Table 5* (page 24) shows reasonably well matched PLOPs and goals. After a few of the GGs, the reader might benefit from covering the goal with a sheet of paper and attempting to write one based on the discussion. After a few more, one might cover the discussion also and try independently to write a measurable goal. Always remember that our measurable goal is that you, the reader:

Will be able on each attempt, to write a measurable goal which contains:

(a) an observable behavior,
(b) a criterion clearly stating how well, how much or at what level the behavior is to be performed and
(c) the given or condition if necessary.

Table

5

Hypothetical PLOPs & Corresponding Goals

PLOP	Goal
1. Reads 4th grade material aloud at 89 wpm.	1. Will read 4th grade material at 140 wpm.
2. Copies words from book at 18 wpm.	2. Will copy words from book at 35 wpm.
3. Writes numerals in random order at 30 npm.	3. Will write numerals in random order at 50 npm.
4. Given written problems, says math fact answers (+, -, x, â) at 42 fpm.	4. Given written problems, will say math fact answers (+, -, x, â) at 70 fpm.
5. Given letter symbols, says corresponding sounds at 20 spm.	5. Given letter symbols, will say corresponding sounds at 50 spm.
6. Writes a story, given story starter, a 6 wpm.	6. Will write a story, given story starter, a 16 wpm.
7. Keyboards at 18 characters per minute.	7. Will keyboard at 50 characters per minute.
8. Ties shoes in 2 minutes.	8. Will tie shoes in 30 seconds.
9. Has 3-4 tantrums per day.	9. Will have zero tantrums per day.
10. Initiates 1-2 peer interactions per day.	10. Will initiate 5 or more peer interactions per day.

Just before we launch into the real world of Gobbledygooks, Table 3 presents seven crucial tips to keep in mind when evaluating GGs and when writing real goals, which are both measurable and to be measured.

Table 3

Tips for Measurable Goal Development

1. Focus a goal on each of the student's important, unique educational needs. For many children, there will be 2 to 5 major needs and, therefore, goals. If the team agrees there are more, perhaps some can be dealt with later, so note this fact on the IEP.

2. Be sure that each goal is properly aligned with its current (not more than a few weeks old) measured present level of performance (PLOP) and that the PLOP appears in the IEP.

3. The amount of progress beyond the PLOP which is projected in the goal should be reasonable, taking into account the child's ability, and assuming appropriate, intensive and effective individualized instruction.

4. Beware of repeating the same goal year after year. If progress is being assessed at least quarterly, as it must be, and it appears the student is not going to meet a goal, something must be changed. That may be the service being provided or the goal itself, if it was perhaps inappropriate to begin with.

5. Every goal must have an observable behavior and a specific criterion against which the performance can be reliably assessed by multiple evaluators.

6. Limit the use of percentage to the very few goals for which it is appropriate, e.g., spelling words when the length of the list is unknown or variable and arithmetic problems when the number of them to be solved varies or is unknown.

7. Above all, measure the child's progress toward the measurable goal. A measurable goal not measured is 100% useless.

From Gobbledygook to Clearly Written IEP Goals

How Not to Write a Goal

(Note: This is a sample of a poorly written goal rendered measurable.)

1. Gobbledygook (GG)

Lenny will improve his behavior 75% of the time.

2. Discussion

This GG contains three major elements — improve, behavior, and 75% of the time and each one demonstrates a major problem, a totally not okay way to write a goal. First, "improve" his behavior is unacceptable because it would require much more information than is provided to know whether Lenny met the goal. We would have to know the beginning "level" of his behavior and how much improvement it would take to constitute "improvement" for the purpose of the goal.

Second, what is "behavior"? Sadly, educators have begun to use the word "behavior" as if it means "inappropriate behavior." This is seen in terminology such as "behavior class" or he has "more behaviors" than he used to. The apparent intent of the GG written here is that Lenny will have fewer inappropriate behaviors, covering less time per day, than he has today. If that's the case, then say so.

Third, what is "75% of the time"? Does it mean it's okay if Lenny's behavior is atrocious 25% of the time? If so, that's 1 to 2 hours during a school day, plus a couple of hours at home. That probably isn't what was meant. Might it mean he will behave properly in 3/4 of the behavioral opportunities he has? But every mini-second of every minute of every hour is a behavioral opportunity. No one could monitor that and certainly not a teacher who has from 5-35 other students to track.

Perhaps "75% of the time" was meant to stand for some kind of "increase" in appropriate behavior. If so, we have the same problem. If his behavior is now appropriate 60% of the time and we are striving for 75%, how would we measure that? What do we record and how often?

This GG is a fine one to drive home the idea that we must be able to **assess what we have set as a goal**. What would one **do** (record, mark, count, etc.), how often, to know if Lenny was "improving his behavior 75% of the time?" Would one have to count every minute (or second) of every hour all day and, for each, judge whether his behavior was or was not improved? Could we do a sample and record every 10th minute of the day? What would we use as the "baseline" against which to assess whether the current behavior was "improved"? Would multiple observers agree?

One moral of this introductory GG is that "X percent of the time" is often difficult to decipher and apply.

3. Goal

By the end of one year, Lenny will have fewer than five inappropriate behaviors per week.

4. Test

The observable behavior targeted in the goal is that behavior which is "inappropriate." We might find some observers occasionally disagreeing about whether a particular behavior is inappropriate, but that is outweighed by the advantage of not having to specify every possible inappropriate behavior. The criterion is fewer than five a week This could easily be tracked by a teacher or aide wearing a strip of masking tape on the back of a hand and simply tallying any inappropriate behaviors of Lenny's. Add three or four strips of tape and behaviors of several students could be similarly tracked.

Timmy Crosses the Street (Maybe)

1. Gobbledygook (GG)

Timmy will cross the street safely 80% of the time.

2. Discussion

This GG passes our test, i.e., it has the observable behavior of crossing the street and a criterion of 80% of the time. Nonetheless, we have an obvious and huge problem. Is it perhaps a failure of common sense? A failure to think about what one has written?

Apparently some one in a position of great authority once upon a time announced to the IEP goal writers of the world that students who receive special education are "80 percenters." The widespread use of 80% in IEP goals and objectives is bizarre at best and diabolical at worst, as in Timmy's case. The writer of Timmy's goal probably did not mean it would be acceptable for Timmy to be hit by a car every fifth time he attempts a street crossing. Yet that is the undeniable and unacceptable implication of the GG as written. Here, one needs to ask, "What would be the result if the goal were met?" Next, what result do we really want? Of course we hope that Timmy will cross the street safely 100% of the time. One might be tempted to include in this goal something like, "Given instruction in the importance of looking both ways twice, Timmy will . . ." However, goals need not include instruction per se. It is always assumed. Since street crossing is an issue for Timmy, it is reasonable to assume he may be a bit away from doing it independently. If the realistic goal is that Timmy cross safely when a supervisor prompts him to look both ways twice, then this condition or "given" can be part of the goal.

Timmy crosses the Street (Maybe)

3. Goal

Given a supervisor's direction to look both ways twice before crossing, Timmy will cross the street safely 100% of the time.

4. Test

The goal passes the test — the behavior of street crossing is observable, the criterion is explicit, and the given is appropriate and necessary for Timmy at this time.

2

Chip and Friends

1. Gobbledygook (GG)

Chip will initiate conversation/comment with peers at lunch given prompts with 80% accuracy.

2. Discussion

This goal is easily repaired because we know precisely what the desired behavior is — initiating conversation with peers. The problem is the meaningless "with 80% accuracy." How in the world could one determine whether an initiation, e.g., "Hi, Joe" is 80% accurate? The use of the phrase "80% accuracy," without possible meaning in this context, reveals that the writer never intended for the behavior to be measured and that is a disturbing revelation, at best. A measurable goal is 100% useless unless it is measured.

The phrase "80% accuracy" gives no clue as to the criterion for success the writer intended, except perhaps to indicate that perfect performance was not sought. We will include our own criterion, which is based on the fact that this is the goal for a full year. Even though Chip is a low performing youngster, it seems reasonable to expect that in a year he will learn to initiate appropriate comments to peers across settings without prompting.

3. Goal

For three consecutive days Chip will initiate at least five appropriate verbal comments/conversations with peers during lunch, recess and other unstructured times.

4. Test

The behavior is initiating conversation, the criterion is five times on each of three consecutive days, and the given is during unstructured times.

3 Andrew's Teeth

1. Gobbledygook

Andrew will, 80% of the time, not bite everyone or approximate [sic] himself in a biting position.

2. Discussion

This goal as written would be successfully met if Andrew spent one full hour (20% of a five-hour day) each school day actively biting his classmates and/or teacher. Is it believable that the writer of the GG really thought that would be acceptable? Probably not. In evaluating a criterion such as "80% of the time" it is often helpful to ask how one might determine whether it had been reached. Here, one might suggest keeping track of the amount of time Andrew spends biting or physically threatening to bite. What if the aide observed for 15 minutes and Andrew didn't bite at all? Goal met? What if in the next 15 minutes Andrew bit four times and threatened to bite twice, but all six incidents combined took only a minute and a half? Success? What is 80% of the time?

Another problem is that to "approximate himself in a biting position" is not totally clear. Perhaps what was meant is that Andrew physically threatens to bite, in addition to actually biting. It is disturbing to see that after a year of behavior shaping, we still expect Andrew to be biting or threatening to bite at all. The rewritten goal reflects a zero biting target. Even if Andrew still reverts to biting on rare occasions, a goal of no biting is still appropriate. School personnel are not legally responsible for a child's failure to achieve a goal, provided progress was regularly assessed and the interventions changed as necessary, based on progress or lack of it.

3. Goal

During the last month of the IEP year, Andrew will not bite anyone or physically threaten to do so.

4. Test

The behavior is biting and the criterion is zero events.

4 | Jason and the Buttons

1. Gobbledygook

Jason will gain three new fine motor skills by June, 2006.

2. Discussion

This goal is very close to acceptable. The language is appropriately plain and straightforward. However, one difficulty is that we don't have a criterion for knowing the developmental level of the desired new skills, nor do we know what counts as one skill. For example, if Jason used a table knife, a fork and a spoon properly, would that be one or three skills? Or if he copied a circle, triangle and square, would that be one or three new skills? How are we to know whether these really are "new" skills? Is Jason like the 6 and a half year old we met recently who is just now working on developing a pincer grasp (closing thumb and index finger), or is he just a slightly klutzy six-year old? In other words, we need to know his present developmental level and his target level.

3. Goal

Jason will attain a six-year-old developmental level in cutting, copying geometric forms and buttoning.

4. Test

The behaviors are cutting, copying and buttoning, and the criterion is a six-year level (as found on any number of developmental scales).

5 Practicality and Exactitude

1. Gobbledygook

Jess will practice prosocial classroom/school behavior 80% of the time by June, 2006.

2. Discussion

The intent here is not to encourage Jess to display antisocial behaviors for 20% of each day or hour. Yet a literal reading of this GG allows exactly that. The term "prosocial" may communicate closely to an in-group that uses it with a precise meaning known to them. However, it does not work well for many readers. For example, if a student is sitting alone and working quietly is that "prosocial?"

Another issue raised by this goal is whether goals should always be framed in terms of positive behaviors. Some say so, pointing out that usually we hope to replace the undesirable behavior with an appropriate one. However, in the context of IDEA, progress assessment is so critical that ease of measurement is a factor sometimes outweighing other considerations. "Once a week" is far easier to track, document and report than "80% of the time."

While our preference in this case is to aim for zero inappropriate behaviors, many are uncomfortable with what they see as an unrealistic expectation. For that reason, the goal below and some others throughout this guide may have a low target rate, rather than zero, for inappropriate behaviors.

3. Goal

Jess will display no more than one inappropriate, antisocial behavior per week by June, 2006.

4. Test

The criterion of one per week is clear. Some might wonder if "inappropriate, antisocial behavior" is observable. Our view is that the overwhelming majority of us can readily recognize what behaviors are included. We know it when we see it, and this is a case where practicality prevails over exactitude.

6 Chip Functions

1. Gobbledygook

Chip will demonstrate improved independent functioning within the classroom as measured by documented teacher observation with 90-100% accuracy.

2. Discussion

What is meant by "improved independent functioning?" If the person who wrote this GG were here, one appropriate question to ask would be, "What would Chip do more or less frequently than he does now that would tell you he had satisfactorily improved independent functioning?" Perhaps the answer would include completing his assignments without assistance, correctly following verbal instructions the teacher gives to the class, or participating appropriately in small group activities. The next question would be, "How often does he do these things now?" A present level of performance is essential when the concern is to make "improvement" or to "increase" a performance. When the goal is stated as a level to be reached, the present level of performance is less crucial, but still mandated by law. In sum, the term "improved independent functioning" has to be translated into observable countable behaviors before a real goal can be written.

A second unknown is to what the "90-100% accuracy" refers? If it refers to the teacher's observations being accurate, it has no role in the goal statement because it would refer to the teacher's behavior, not the students's behavior. Proper goals focus on the student's behaviors, not on that of others. Furthermore, as seen in hearing decisions quoted earlier, teacher observation, by itself, is **not** an adequate objective assessment.

A significant amount of observation /documentation would be necessitated by using a 9 out of 10 trials translation of the GG's original 90%. Four of four consecutive trials might be as effective and more manageable. Because every goal must be measurable and measured, we may sometimes deliberately minimize the measurement effort required, to help insure that progress is actually assessed.

3. Goal

Chip will follow the teacher's classroom directions without repetition or assistance (4 out of 5 times), complete class assignments without undue assistance (5 of 5 times), and participate in small group activities, when assigned to do so by the teacher, with no inappropriate behaviors (4 of 5 times) during the last grading period of the IEP year.

4. Test

The observable behaviors and objective criteria are present.

7 Let's be Social

1. Gobbledygook

J.R. will form appropriate social relationships with peers and teachers 4 of 5 times.

2. Discussion

The person who wrote this GG many well have had a clear idea of the behaviors implicit in "appropriate social relationships." The otherwise clean, direct language of the GG suggests this may be so. However, each of us might have a somewhat different idea of the specific behaviors that indicate "appropriate social relationships."

A second common problem is what constitutes a "time" during which an appropriate social relationship might be formed. So, although on its face this GG seems straightforward, the prospect of actually measuring whether the child has attained the goal is troubling. Imagine what you would do, given the assignment of determining whether J.R. had or had not formed appropriate social relationships with peers and teachers 4 of 5 times. What if, at first blush, it appears he has no positive relationships with peers, but has several with teachers? Does the "and" between peers and teachers mean that at least some (if so, how many) of these relationships must be with peers and some with teachers? Lest these questions seem like nit-picking we should remind ourselves that IDEA demands that goals be measurable and measured. With this GG the best we can do is to "suppose" what behaviors might have been meant and what "4 of 5 times" might mean.

3. Goal

Between June 10 and June 20, 2006, J.R. will interact appropriately with peers and/or teachers at least 10 times more frequently than he interacts inappropriately with them.

4. Test

The goal is better than the GG, but is not perfect. It could be difficult to count the appropriate interactions without further definition of "appropriate interaction." If that were resolved, the criterion would then be adequate, but would require a significant effort to assess it. Perhaps the reader can write a similar, but more practical, manageable goal.

8 Cart Before the Horse?

1. Gobbledygook

Keenan will increase his reading comprehension/critical thinking skills by one-half year by utilizing decoding strategies.

2. Discussion

Keenan is an eighth grader whose reading comprehension is at about fifth grade level. He scored at the 1st percentile on the WIAT Reading subtest. No present level of performance on his IEP is at all related to his critical thinking skills. Keenan is now about three years behind his grade level in reading comprehension. If this present GG were met, he would then be three and one half years behind grade level. This is not an acceptable target.

Whether "utilizing decoding strategies" is effective for the purpose of improving reading comprehension is open to discussion. Our view is that fluent decoding is a prerequisite to comprehension and that until it is achieved, fluent decoding, not comprehension, should be the primary goal. The GG as written seems to suggest that less-than-adequate decoding is the reason for Keenan's comprehension lag. If so, the focus of the goal should be on fluent decoding. However, we will accept the intent to write a goal for reading comprehension. Critical thinking is important in many more activities than just reading, and it should have a separate goal written.

3. Goal

Given 7th grade expository material to read silently, Keenan will correctly answer 95% of a variety of comprehension questions over that material.

4. Test

The behavior is answering questions, the criterion is 95% of answers correct, and the given is 7th grade expository material.

9

Andrew and the clock

1. Gobbledygook

Andrew will, with 80% accuracy, tell time to the hour.

2. Discussion

Is it useful to tell time to the hour? This GG seems to perhaps have been born from the writer's lack of a tried and true method of teaching more precise time telling. There is also a question raised by the fact that Andrew's developmental level is about that of a two to three year-old child. Is time telling a priority for him? However, if we assume telling time to the hour is a reasonable and appropriate goal for him, we still have to deal with the ubiquitous 80% accuracy.

If the time, to the nearest hour, were 10:00, but Andrew said it was 9:00, would that meet the 80% accuracy standard? How would you calculate that? Once again, 80% fails us, Andrew, and his IEP. Since telling time to the hour from a digital clock is an altogether different skill from reading an analog clock, the goal must be clear as to which is to be taught.

3. Goal

Given 10 pictures of analog clock faces, Andrew will correctly state the time to the nearest hour on 9 of them.

4. Test

The behavior is stating the time, clock faces are the given and the criterion is 9 out of 10 correct. Perhaps the GG writer intended the 80% accuracy to mean 8 out of 10 clock faces would be read correctly. If so, that is what should have been written.

10 What?

1. Gobbledygook

Kelly will increase his knowledge of the conventions of language and text to construct meaning by one grade level by the next annual IEP.

2. Discussion

Too many efforts at goal writing, including this one, are driven by the concept of "standards-based IEPs." In this approach to writing IEP goals, a state standard designed for regular education students is used as the basis for a child's IEP goals. This approach does not take into account two critical facts. First, the IEP is supposed to deal with the **special education** and services the child needs, not with the regular curriculum. IDEA requires that the child have the special education services needed to **access** the general curriculum. These services need to be on the IEP, but the general curriculum does not need to be on the IEP, nor should it be.

Secondly, the IEP is to be an individualized program. This individualization must be reflected in the IEP goals, as well as in the services. State standards for all regular education students are the opposite of individualized goals for special education students. Once we recognize standards for the vague umbrella statements they are, we can begin to write meaningful, measurable plain language goals. Then if we are required to show how a goal is standard-driven as is required by some districts, one can always find a standard under which any goal can be subsumed, because standards are so vague, broad and fuzzy. To work the other direction, as the author of this GG did — from a standard to a goal — is inevitably a failure.

Even if the concept of a standards-based IEP were not totally flawed, this particular standard, with all due respect, is a marvelous example of gobbledygook. This special education student, who is 10 years old and reads at about a second grade level, is to **improve** (by one grade level) **his knowledge** of the **conventions of language and text**. His purpose for doing this is to **construct meaning**. Goals should be written so that ordinary folk, such as parents and the rest of us, can easily know and agree what is meant. What are "conventions of text?" And don't most of us still believe we derive meaning from what we read rather than making it up or constructing?

Often its short term objectives give clues as to what the GG means. Kelly's IEP contained two objectives to lead to reaching this goal. The objectives were that Kelly would decode second and third grade word lists with 90% accuracy, and that he would "Increase his fluency on four of five occasions with 80% accuracy when reading a book at his level." The first objective is understandable and arguably reasonable, although the 90% level of decoding accuracy is unacceptably low. The second objective of increasing fluency on four of five occasions with 80% accuracy is difficult to understand. Suppose Kelly had these daily scores[1] while reading aloud from a book at his reading level: (a) 60 wpm/12Errors, (b) 75 wpm/14E, (c) 68 wpm/2E, (d) 72 wpm/8E, (e) 80 wpm/23E, and (f) 79 wpm/20E. Did he or did he not meet the two objectives? How do we know? Is there a better way to phrase the objective so we could more readily determine whether he had met it?

3. Goal

Given a fourth grade book, Kelly will read aloud at a rate of 90 wpm with no more than 2 errors.

4. Test

This goal is a common model for oral reading objectives. Clearly it contains the necessary observable behavior, criterion and given.

---

[1]Words correct per minute (wcpm) is a standard fluency measure for oral reading. Some prefer to use total words per minute (wpm) and errors per minute, as we have done here.

The Spotted owl

1. Gobbledygook

Andrew will name 10 endangered animals.

2. Discussion

This appears to be a perfectly appropriate goal. It is written simply and directly and is easily measurable. The only obvious question that might be raised is whether this is worthy of being an annual goal. Perhaps better if it were one of many smaller objectives. But leaving that aside, there is a far more important, but hidden problem. Twelve-year old Andrew's present levels of performance show that his speech/language development is estimated at a 13-24 month level. He does not respond to questions. Naming 10 endangered animals may be a fine objective for some children, but not for Andrew at this point in time. This GG apparently came from the standards-based approach. Perhaps the science teacher was required to find a science standard for Andrew and animals seemed to be one of the easiest topics in the standards. This GG can not be salvaged, only changed.

3. Goal

Given pictures of common objects (e.g., toys, animals), Andrew will name them, performing expressively at a 3 to 4-year old level. Given a receptive language task such as pointing to the picture of a named object, e.g., "Point to the tree," he will perform at a 3 to 4-year old level.

4. Test

Naming and pointing are common observable behaviors and a developmental level (3 to 4-year old level here) can be an acceptable criterion, especially when such norms are readily available in a variety of valid sources including standardized tests such as the Peabody Picture Vocabulary Test (receptive vocabulary).

Turn it off, Please

I. Gobbledygook

Andrew will be able to conserve water and electricity and to recycle paper. (This GG seems to confirm the science-teacher hypothesis on Andrew's previous GG.)

2. Discussion

Since Andrew functions at a 2 to 3 year old developmental level in non-language areas, the primary issue is what he can do to demonstrate learning in these important aspects of conservation. The GG as written, could apply to most every one on the planet, but there would be many different ways of performing the goal. Our question is how might this child with his functional level of 2 to 3 years of age demonstrate his ability to perform these conservation activities.

3. Goals

1. When prompted, Andrew will turn off water faucets after using them, every time.

2. With one prompt, Andrew will place used paper in the correct recycling container on 9 of 10 opportunities.

4. Test

Each goal has its own observable behavior (turning off faucet, tossing paper) and its own criterion (every time, 9 of 10 opportunities). Combining these into one goal proved difficult and confusing. These goals, like his "endangered animals" goal seem more like objectives. They are hardly important enough to be high priority annual goals.

13 What's for Dinner?

1. Gobbledygook

Kelly will practice health-enhancing behaviors and reduce health risks.

2. Discussion

This GG tells us little beyond a general, broad direction in which to look for the writer's intent. Often when a goal is this vague, some clue can be gained about intent from the objectives. Not so, in this case, as the single objective deals with strategies for coping with stress and strong feelings.

This GG like too many others was taken verbatim from state standards. Hopefully no further indication of the foolishness of this practice is needed.

As far as his extensive records reveal, Kelly had no special needs related to health or to health risks, and therefore, no such goal should be proposed for him. However, for the sake of discussion, let us suppose he did have a need in this area.

3. Goal

Given a list of common foods, or a restaurant menu, Kelly will select three each nutritiously sound breakfasts, lunches and dinners, and he will identify 10 major foods or food combinations he must avoid.

4. Test

This goal requires two related behaviors (identifying "good "and "bad" foods), and the criteria are (a) nutritiously sound and (b) to be avoided (as determined by his parents and doctor and made known to the school).

14 Understand the Day

1. Gobbledygook

Adriana will increase her understanding of a structured home/school day, by participating in routines and activities from a verbally and physically assisted level to an imitative or verbally prompted level by April, 2005.

2. Discussion

What does "increase her understanding of a structured home/school day" mean? How might you and I increase our understanding of a day? The implication is that by "participating in routines and activities" at a different level, this will occur. Presently Adriana participates at a "verbally and physically assisted level." By April, she will participate at an "imitative or verbally prompted" level. What is the difference between an "assisted" and a "verbally prompted" level. What is the difference between "verbally assisted" and "verbally prompted" participation? And where does an "imitative level" fit in with "assisted" and "prompted?"

After recognizing that the language in this GG complicates the effort, one possible approach to clarifying it is to visualize an activity that might allow Adriana to demonstrate her increased understanding of a day. Suppose the routine is that the children come into the room, place their backpacks in cubbies (labeled by name and color), and then go to their assigned (by color and animal name) group area. Perhaps the GG tells us that presently Adriana needs verbal and physical assistance to do this. The GG then might mean that she could perform this routine by watching/following/imitating a classmate.

3. Goal

Given four daily classroom routines (e.g., lining up for recess, putting away materials at the end of the day), Adriana will correctly perform them by imitating classmates or with no more than one verbal prompt by an adult.

4. Test

This goal is performing routines, the givens are four routines and verbal prompts, and the criterion is "correctly."

15 Speak Up

1. Gobbledygook

Adriana will increase her understanding and use of formal language by responding to and using words to express herself, given models and verbal/physical assistance as needed 80% of the time by April, 2005.

2. Discussion

Parsing this GG reveals that what Adriana will be doing is "responding to and using words to express herself." To what does "80% of the time" refer? Grammar does not answer this. It might mean responding to/using words 80% of the time or to be given assistance 80% of the time. Or not. What is 80% of the time? Four out of five hours? Four days out of five?

One plain reading of this GG suggests that Adriana presently does not use words to express herself. However, one of the short-term objectives on her IEP is that Adriana will describe an action in sentences, e.g., "I put the boots on the bottom shelf." If she does not presently use words to express herself, it is hard to imagine that an eight word sentence would be an intermediate objective en route to the goal. Two of the other objectives for this GG require Adriana to "read words." That might be because the IEP says the state standard to which this GG relates is "To use strategies within the reading process to construct meaning."

One reasonable guess as to what this GG writer might have intended is that Adriana does not yet express herself verbally at an age appropriate level and that, therefore, the goal is that her verbal expression moves measurably closer to that age-appropriate level.

3. Goal

Adriana will use at least 10 four-word or longer spontaneous utterances daily.

4. Test

The behavior is speaking and the criterion is 10 four-word utterances daily. The strip of masking tape on the back of the hand would work very well to tally the occurrence of 4 word or longer utterances.

Three

1. Gobbledygook

Adriana will increase her understanding of how to use numbers and quantities to a spontaneous level by April, 2005.

2. Discussion

The key to this writer's intent seems to be that Adriana will "use numbers and quantities." The problem is that this could refer to anything from asking for more ice cream to solving astrophysics problems. The short term IEP objectives reveal she will learn to count to 20, recognize bigger/smaller, more/less and learn number-numeral correspondences to 10. Without those objectives, one could only speculate about what the goal means and could not possibly evaluate whether Adriana has achieved it. This vague and not measurable goal can only be understood by examining its short-term objectives. Now that IDEA 2004 no longer requires short-term objectives (except for the lowest performing third or so of special education students), it may be that we will see more unclear goals like this but without the objectives to help decipher them.

3. Goal

Adriana will be able to (a) perform single digit addition and subtraction with 90% accuracy, (b) count to 100 without assistance with no more than 2 errors and (c) use manipulatives to solve problems requiring addition/subtraction with quantities up to 20 with 90% accuracy.

4. Test

These three related goals all have observable behaviors and criteria. The original GG may have intended for "spontaneous level" to be a criterion, but in this context it is not. The first and third goals illustrate the rare appropriate uses for a percent of accuracy. Spelling words is another example where a percentage may be useful. The use of multiple goals packaged together may raise questions. However, this technique may occasionally be necessary and appropriate, especially for those IEPs where short-term objectives are no longer used.

Some districts have required IEP teams to write goals with this format: "Johnny will improve in X as shown by mastery of the short term objectives." Whether this qualifies as a measurable annual goal may be debated, but if a district which is using the format stops including short term objectives on most IEPs, we may see a move toward multiple goals such as this one. Ultimately, the courts may determine whether such a format is legally acceptable.

17 OUCh!

1. Gobbledygook

Adriana will develop knowledge and use of functional science related to her environment from the verbally/physically prompted level to an independent level by April, 2006.

2. Discussion

Imagine that Adriana's school has selected you to assess whether Adriana has met the goal above. No further information is available to you. What would you do to ascertain whether Adriana has "knowledge and use of functional science at an independent level?" Would it ever occur to you that the actual target behavior of this goal was that Adriana would learn to look out the window and state, 80% of the time, whether it was sunny, rainy, cloudy or windy? That was, in fact, the single objective for the goal. This appears to be yet another example of someone mistakenly believing that the regular education, standards-driven curriculum must appear on the IEP. The fact is that the IEP is to address the child's unique needs, and this child had no unique need to name weather conditions.

A unique need in the area of science is somewhat difficult to imagine. While it may be a bit far-fetched, suppose Adriana lives in an area where there are many poisonous or otherwise dangerous insects and other such critters. Further suppose Adriana has an intense interest in all manner of animals and creepy crawlies and has a very underdeveloped awareness of danger. Her goal must be changed to reflect her real world.

3. Goal

Given pictures of each of the dangerous "critters" in the region, each with four distractors, Adriana will point to or name the dangerous ones with 100% accuracy.

4. Test

The behavior is pointing or naming and the criterion is 100%.

Write, Wrote, Written

1. Gobbledygook

Tyler will write using various forms to communicate a variety of purposes and audiences.

2. Discussion

The sad irony is that Tyler, a high school student, has a disability in writing and his parents' primary concern is that he learn compensatory strategies for writing. Yet, this totally vague and non-measurable "anything goes" GG is supposed to guide his special education services. Suppose one were assigned the task of writing a goal so broad and so vague that anything written by anyone could be claimed to meet the goal. To do better than this GG would be difficult, if not impossible.

Occasionally, as we have seen, the short term objectives can provide meaningful direction when the goal fails to, as here. However, these were the objectives for this GG: (1) Write to reflect on learning; (2) Write to communicate and report information from research; (3) Write for problem solving and application; (4) Write using forms appropriate to purpose and topic. Obviously, these provide little help.

To prepare a meaningful writing goal for Tyler requires that we first learn about his present level of writing. It is also essential that we fully consider alternative or compensating strategies, as the parents wish. Alternatives to writing may be absolutely essential, depending on whether proven effective methods/programs in the hands of experienced, qualified persons already have been tried. Such methods/programs do exist, and if they have not yet been properly used with Tyler, such should be done before completely subordinating his own writing potential to alternatives.

The best information available about Tyler's present level in writing (which was also available to the GG writer) is this: "Tyler needs to write simple sentence, contextual conventions . . . improve in the conventions of writing (punctuation, spelling, and application) through proofreading and revision . . . [to be] exposed to a variety of writing genres, i.e., diaries, journals, captions for pictures to assist in written products." This information is still not totally helpful, so we must, for our purpose, add details that may or may not be totally accurate, but which would have been available to the original IEP developers.

Assume that with prompting Tyler writes simple declarative sentences (average length of seven words) with no major errors and, thereby, demonstrates his mastery of basic conventions of spelling, punctuation and capitalization at about a beginning third grade level. He is now almost 16 years old, is in 10th grade, and has average intelligence. He has roughly two years in which to learn to express his ideas in writing.

3. Goal

Tyler will write and edit a composition of at least five paragraphs, each containing at least a main idea and two supporting ideas. The composition will have no more than two errors of convention.

4. Test

Writing and editing are observable behaviors, and the criteria are spelled out.

Who Dood it?

1. Gobbledygook

When writing single sentences, J. will apply writing rules appropriately and edit his work in 4 of 5 trials.

2. Discussion

This is not measurable because it has no criterion for successful performance of either the writing or the editing. No two evaluators would necessarily agree as to whether J. had accomplished the goal. Suppose his performance was:

Simple Sentence	J.'s Edit
1. He run.	He runned
2. dog sits.	A dog sits
3. I went	I went.
4. Does it.	does it?
5. She jumps	she jumps.

Did J. successfully "apply writing rules and edit his work in 4 of 5 trials" — and what is the basis for your conclusion ? Would a hearing officer agree with you?

3. Goal

J. will write 10 simple sentences of his own choosing, making no more than 5 total errors in grammar, spelling, punctuation and capitalization. When asked to edit those sentences, he will find and correct 90% of his errors.

4. Test

The behavior is writing sentences, and the criterion is successful editing of 90% of any errors made.

3 x 4 = 34

1. Gobbledygook

Given single digit multiplication problems up to 20, J. will complete with 80% accuracy.

2. Discussion

What is included in "single digit multiplication problems up to 20?" If this means the result of the multiplication is up to 20, then 9 x 2 would be included, but 7 x 3 would not be. That seems less than logical. On the other hand, if it means all single digit problems (such as 9 x 8 and 6 x 7) can be solved, then why say "up to 20" since 10 to 20 are not included in single digits? Furthermore, no fluency criterion is provided in the goal. Given 10 single digit multiplication problems, may J. take 30 seconds or 30 minutes to complete them? Surely that matters. Additionally, is it reasonable to settle for 80% accuracy in the basic number facts which are the foundation for all further calculations?

3. Goal

Given a worksheet of 40 single-digit multiplication problems, J. will write answers at the rate of 80 numerals per minute with no more than 2 errors.

4. Test

Writing answers is an observable behavior and 80 numerals per minute is a criterion. A very strong case can be made that all measurable goals should include a fluency criterion as this one does, but that is for another discussion, after we master goal writing with any reasonable and measurable criteria.

1. Gobbledygook

J. will increase his social skills with no more than one prompt on 4 consecutive recording periods.

2. Discussion

"Increase his social skills" is so broad and general as to be impossible to decipher or assess. Further, if the goal is to increase or improve something, it is essential that the starting point be known. Otherwise, how could one tell whether the level reached at the end of the year was an improvement? The exception to this is that if the goal says "Will improve to X level," then reaching X is sufficient without knowing the beginning level. However, the word "improve" is not necessary — better to just say "reach X level."

Either one of these problems — the vagueness of "social skills" or the absence of knowing how much improvement is required in what behavior — is sufficient to render the goal meaningless gobbledygook. If the goal writer were here, we could ask exactly which social behaviors were of concern. Perhaps the answer would be something like "J. is so shy he never approaches or greets other children. He just sits by himself at recess and lunch."

3. Goal

J. will initiate three positive peer interactions daily on 3 of 4 consecutive days.

4. Test

The behavior is initiating positive interactions, and the criterion is three daily on 3 of 4 days.

22 | Dress and feed

1. Gobbledygook

Paul will demonstrate age-appropriate life skills and behaviors to foster independent living.

2. Discussion

This GG is even less appropriate than it may appear. Paul was 10 years old when the GG was written, and he was functioning at about a 2-year old level in all areas. To suggest that in one year he could function at his chronological age level and be on his way to independent living is non-professional at best. We can never rule out a miracle, but to suggest to parents that this would, in fact, occur is worse than thoughtless. In recent years, special education has been guilty of deliberately using euphemisms that obscure rather than reveal truths. Setting totally unrealistic goals also misleads parents and results in disappointment, frustration, disillusionment and worse. As in so many other goals we've seen, the language in this one is so broad we can only guess what might have been meant by "life skills and behaviors to foster independent living."

3. Goal

Paul will dress himself independently, except for buttoning and tying, within three minutes when clothes are laid out for him. He will also feed himself except for cutting and spreading food.

4. Test

Dressing and feeding are observable behaviors. The implicit criteria are in the ordinary meaning of "dressing and feeding" himself, minus the exceptions.

23 Useless, 80% of the Time

1. Gobbledygook

Ryder will improve his language by using/listening to complete sentences 80% of the time.

2. Discussion

One of the basic principals of goal writing is that the instruction to be provided to enable the learner to reach the goal is assumed and not included in the goal. If "using/listening to complete sentences" is the instruction to be provided, that should not be included in the goal. The "80% of the time" must be intended to modify "improve his language" since it would be impossible to "use/listen to complete sentences" 80% of the time. In all probability, "80% of the time" was gratuitously added because someone had taught the goal writer to tack that on to every goal in the false belief that doing so would create measurability.

This analysis leaves us with "Ryder will improve his language" as the crux of the GG. This could mean that Ryder learns to say "mama," "dada" and "baba" or that Ryder edits doctoral dissertations to eliminate dangling participles. It is fair to say this goal is 100% totally and completely useless. We can only guess what might be a real and appropriate goal for Ryder.

3. Goal

When asked to point to pictures of everyday objects in his environment, such as common animals, Ryder correctly points to at least 50. When asked to name (what is this?) the pictures, he will correctly name 30.

4. Test

This goal encompasses both receptive (point to) and expressive (name) language behaviors with criteria of 50 and 30 objects, respectively.

24 Get Real

1. Gobbledygook

Sarah will increase her ability to fluently read grade appropriate texts within one year.

2. Discussion

Sarah is in the fifth grade and is currently reading at a kindergarten level. She is 10 years old and her recent cognitive ability score was below the 0.1 percentile, i.e., she scored lower than 999 of 1,000 students. Is it realistic to suppose she can gain six years of reading skills in one year? Although another way to look at this situation is that Sarah currently has no ability to "fluently read grade-appropriate texts," so that arguably, if she learned fifty new sight words such as "then" and "where," she would be able to read a fifth grade book "more fluently" even though still totally inadequately, non-fluently and with zero comprehension. But surely no serious goal writer would intend to claim that result as success. Given her present reading level and low intellectual ability, even a modest goal of approaching first grade fluency would be optimistic.

3. Goal

Given beginning first grade level material, Sarah will read orally at least 50 words correct per minute and will correctly identify 95% of the Dolch "Easy 110" sight words within 3 minutes.

4. Test

The behaviors in this dual goal are reading text aloud and saying sight words. The criteria are 30 cwpm in oral reading and 95% of 110 sight words read correctly in 3 minutes.

25 | The Cube and the Mammal

1. Gobbledygook

Blake will demonstrate understanding of new vocabulary words and spoken information, follow oral directions, and express himself clearly and meaningfully 80% of the time.

2. Discussion

Does 80% of the time modify understanding new words, following directions, and/or expressing himself? Does it mean he will succeed in 80% of his attempts to do those three things? Are his new vocabulary words to be the names of colors or words like homunculus and propitiate? Superficially this GG sounds pretty good, but examination shows it is totally unmeasurable. Just as we have no idea what would constitute success in understanding vocabulary, so we don't know whether the directions Blake is to follow are more like "Sit down, please" or "Put the tab marked B under notch E unless D is a double dot, and then place tab A under notch C."

As is true of every GG we've looked at in this little guide, a good way to evaluate any proposed goal is to ask yourself, "Exactly what would I do to determine whether the student had met the goal?" Another good question to ask is, "Do I believe that if three of my colleagues were given access to the student and this goal with no further information, would all three come to the same conclusion as to whether the student had reached the goal?"

3. Goal

Given simple directions using newly learned vocabulary such as "Put the red cube [new vocabulary word] on the picture of the mammal [new word]," Blake will follow 90% of all the directions correctly.

4. Test

The behavior is following directions and the criterion is 90% followed correctly. Once again, this illustrates that percentage correct can occasionally be a useful and appropriate criterion. However, it is too often not used appropriately, as we've seen. One might wonder why not say "9 of 10 trials or 4 of 5 opportunities." These are indeed useful and appropriate, sometimes. In this particular situation 90% gives more freedom than specifying a number of trials. Perhaps 5 trials are sufficient to show Blake can readily do it. Perhaps 10, 15 or 20 are needed.

26 | Stop that!

1. Gobbledygook

Kyle will demonstrate respect to others and work cooperatively as a group member.

2. Discussion

To even begin to translate this GG into a measurable, real goal, we must look at Kyle's actual behaviors as shown in his present level of performance in his IEP:

Kyle's inattentiveness and distractibility interfere with his listening and writing ... His impulsive behaviors can also be seen in his need to talk, and he often interrupts others as a result. Kyle experiences sudden mood changes and causes concern when he exhibits anger and frustration primarily in response to social situations. His outbursts are manifested both verbally and physically. Adult intervention is needed to subdue him and redirect his actions to more appropriate responses.

His behaviors range from sitting and listening to a teacher's directions appropriately, to behaving inappropriately with another student (verbal arguments, whacking the other student on the head with his fist) and speaking out defiantly to an adult aide ("I don't want to sit down!" "I don't want to!"). He lashes out at both students and adults, often threatening violence and or grabbing or pushing others.

Kyle's IEP goal raises a familiar issue: Should we target the inappropriate verbal and physical aggression or focus solely on the desired replacement behaviors, as the GG does? "Demonstrate respect for others" and "work cooperatively" are both subject to nearly unlimited interpretation. Each of us knows what behaviors these terms mean to us, but others may think of different sets of behaviors. Observers are more likely to agree that a given behavior is disrespectful than that another behavior is respectful. For this reason, as well as ease and practicality of tracking and measuring, the goal is written in terms of reducing the inappropriate behaviors specifically referred to in Kyle's present level of performance.

3. Goal

Kyle will display each of the following behaviors no more frequently than do his classmates: Verbally interrupting others who are speaking, grabbing or pushing others, having inappropriate verbal or physical outbursts or making threats.

4. Test

Behaviors can be added to or subtracted from the goal as appropriate. There are times when using "what ordinarily happens" as the criterion, as done here, may be acceptable. Perhaps attendance is an even better example, e.g., the student will have no more unexcused absences (or tardies) than is the average for the school. There are other times when only a zero target makes sense. That case can certainly be made here. We went with the class average here because of familiarity with Kyle's class and a belief that a zero target, at least initially, is unrealistic. The target can also be lowered as Kyle progresses.

27 Meaningful?

1. Gobbledygook

Given writing on a topic, Stan will communicate meaning to a reader at least 75% of the occurrences.

2. Discussion

This GG seems to mean that Stan will write things and that three fourths of the time when he does so, what he has written will be meaningful to a reader. A first step is to straighten out the convoluted writing of the writer who wrote Stan's writing goal. The given in this GG does not make sense. A better version could be, "When Stan writes, three out of four of his written messages will be understandable to a reader." This is an improvement in that it is direct and clear. However, it does not have a criterion by which to judge success. If he wrote four single words such as "clap," "stand," "sit" and "smile," and the reader did all but smile, has Stan accomplished the goal? Or must he write understandable directions for expanding the binomial and, thereby, demonstrate the derivation of the normal curve? We must have an objective criterion against which to assess his performance.

Suppose we wish to see Stan write at a solid fourth grade level within the year. Then the goal might include a criterion such as writing a paragraph of 4 to 6 sentences each on three topics in his social studies (or science) text.

The next task is to operationalize "communicate meaning to the reader." Is the reader a first grader who can only read "a," "an", and "the," or is it Stan's teacher who knows Stan and his writing very well? Furthermore, how is the evaluator to know whether the reader got the meaning Stan intended? Does that matter?

3. Goal

Given four grade level appropriate topics, Stan will write a paragraph of at least four meaningful sentences each (as judged by peers) on 3 of the 4 topics.

4. Test

"As judged by peers" (or teachers) is a criterion that we might wish to avoid when possible. When, as here, the descriptor "meaningful" seems to be an important element in the criterion, it is logical to specify meaningful to whom.

Stan's IEP had two more closely related GGs we designate GG_B and GG_C and treat briefly below.

1. GG_B: Given writing on a topic, Stan will elaborate meaning with details at least 75% of the occurrences.

2. Discussion: Like Stan's preceding goal — this one also suffers from convoluted, inexact language. Stan isn't to be given writing on a topic; he is to write on a topic — a very different state of affairs. A translation somewhat like that of his first GG would clarify it.

3. Goal: Given four topic or main idea sentences, Stan will provide four appropriate elaborations/details for 3 of the 4 sentences.

1. GG_C: Stan will write an original writing piece that gives a sense of completeness at least 80% of the occurrences.

2. Discussion: The key idea in this GG appears to be "a sense of completeness." This can readily be operationalized as a beginning, middle and end, or an introduction, body and conclusion (or other similar words depending on the type of writing).

3. Goal: When asked to write five reports on appropriate topics of interest (stories), 4 of 5 of Stan's reports will contain an identifiable introduction, body and conclusion.

28 School Daze

1. Gobbledygook

To increase Nelson's interpersonal skills.

2. Discussion

Oh, dear, whose non-goal is this? Who will increase Nelson's skills? Perhaps the social worker, psychologist, or teacher. In any event, it isn't even written as if it is Nelson's goal. The usual format for this kind of non-goal would be "Nelson will increase his ..."

This GG has none of the characteristics of a goal. It is not something the student will do — it is up to someone else to do it. It contains no observable behaviors and no indication of the level to which "it" (whatever it is) is to be done. As a goal, it is a total failure.

In reality, Nelson is so anxious in social situations that he has refused to go to school for several months. It seems that getting back to school would be a good start and perhaps an essential one. Ideally, it will not take a full year to get Nelson to return to school, so this might not be perfectly suited to be an annual goal. But it is so important that it should be written on the IEP and major efforts focused on it.

When it is accomplished another goal can be added.

3. Goal

Nelson will attend school with no more unexcused absences than other students' average absences.

4. Test

The behavior is to attend school and the criterion is the same attendance level as other students average.

29 | Let's Connect

1. Gobbledygook

While reading a story, Stan will make connections between prior knowledge and the text 70% of the time.

2. Discussion

Just for fun, let us accept this as written and look at how we might determine whether Stan had accomplished it. Whatever we do to assess it must be done while Stan is reading. We might ask him to raise his hand each time he makes a connection between something he is reading and something he already knows. We count the hand raisings during the reading of a 1,000 word passage and find 17. Or maybe he raised his hand 998 times and explained, "I already know all the words except two." Is either a performance that meets the goal? Are both? This approach clearly won't do. Perhaps asking him to make a checkmark in the margin (lightly, in pencil, of course) when something he reads causes him to think about something from his life would work better. However, we still have the problem of how many checkmarks would satisfy the goal. Does the "70% of the time" help? Would that mean that in 7 out of 10 stories he reads, one connection to his prior experience is sufficient and none is necessary for the other three? Or possibly he must connect with 7 of every 10 sentences? Or 7 of every 10 events? Does it matter if the story is a fantasy about aliens in a bizarre, imaginary environment doing unheard of things versus a story about a boy of Stan's age, interests, and background? Of course it does.

3. Goal

After reading a story that contains references to at least 10 activities or places familiar to him (e.g., riding a bike, going to the mall), Stan will be able to relate a brief personal connection to 70% of the familiar references.

4. Test

Relating (telling) is the behavior; the criterion is 70% of the familiar references.

I Would Like You to Meet

1. Gobbledygook

Fred will develop behavioral, emotional and social skills with 85% accuracy.

2. Discussion

What behavior(s) is Fred to do which will show he has mastered this GG? The fact is that we can't tell what behaviors are expected, so it would be impossible to evaluate whether he had accomplished them. Suppose the GG writer had specified a social skill such as properly introducing people to each other — friends, parents, or teachers. Then the next question would be whether the criterion of 85% accuracy is appropriate. If Fred introduced a friend of his to his favorite teacher, how would we judge how "accurately" he did it? If we knew what accuracy in an introduction meant, how would we determine an exact percentage of accuracy? Might the writer have meant that if Fred did 10 introductions, he would do eight and a half of them correctly or appropriately? Is it even possible that the writer simply uses 85% accuracy to mean that Fred will do pretty well at introducing folks, but we don't expect perfection?

Another question is whether mastering introductions is important enough to justify it being an annual goal. However, we'll use it for illustration and then add a related goal of somewhat larger magnitude. To make this GG into an acceptable goal, one must supply both an observable behavior and a meaningful criterion.

3. Goal 1

Fred will introduce people of various ages and backgrounds to each other with no more than one breach of acceptable protocol in 10 introductions.

Goal 2

During an unstructured time, such as lunch, Fred will have at least two appropriate conversations of five or more exchanges each with two different people.

4. Test

The behaviors are introducing folks and having conversational exchanges. The criteria are clear, and both goals are, therefore, measurable.

31 What Say?

I. Gobbledygook

Nelson will improve his ability to speak clearly to communicate meaning.

2. Discussion

This GG doesn't tell us how to assess Nelson's "ability to speak clearly to communicate meaning." Are we to look for progress in articulation, grammar and/or semantics? One of Nelson's short-term objectives for this goal is to "be able to ask questions with verbal prompts for clarification." Few would have supposed that asking questions would be a major factor in speaking clearly.

When we eliminate from this GG all the words that add nothing, we are left with "Nelson will speak [more] clearly." Perhaps it is easier now to see that this goal is very inadequate. The behavior is "speaking," but there is no way to know how well or to what level of proficiency Nelson must speak in order to accomplish the goal. Many of us would assume that when someone needs to speak more clearly, the issue is articulation. However, in this case, another objective listed for Nelson, in addition to asking questions, was to translate his thoughts into complete sentences 25% of the time.

Nelson's present level of performance reveals that he is "unable to make conversation with more than one word," and sometimes "he does not speak clearly enough to be understood." Also he reads pre-K books which belong to his sister. Putting this background information together makes it possible to write an appropriate goal.

3. Goal

Nelson will orally answer 9 of 10 questions (to which he knows the answers, e.g., "What are you wearing now?"), using at least three meaningful and understandable words in each answer.

4. Test

The behavior to be observed is giving oral responses. The given is "questions to which he knows the answers." The criterion is that his response to 9 of 10 questions must be understandable, meaningful, and contain at least three words.

32 over Alicia's Head

1. Gobbledygook

With cues and prompts, Alicia will accurately interpret figurative language phrases and make appropriate inferences in material read or listened to on 3 of 5 opportunities.

2. Discussion

Alicia reads at a beginning second grade level and her listening comprehension is at about that level or slightly higher. Presently, her "interpretive" and "inferential" abilities are somewhat like those of a 7-year old. A reasonable target could be an increase to that of a 9-year old or to a fourth grade level. What kind of figurative language phrases do fourth graders interpret, and what kinds of inferences do they make? Even more important to ask is what interpretative and inferential language skills are vital for someone operating linguistically at about a second grade level? Are there other related skills, such as reading and vocabulary development that might precede this GG? In other words, this GG is not properly matched to Alicia's present levels of performance.

3. Goal

Given five examples of figurative phrases (vocabulary pre-taught, if unfamiliar) selected from a fourth grade reader and five inferential questions from the same material read aloud to her, Alicia will correctly explain/answer 8 of the 10 phrases/questions.

4. For the few remaining GG Goals in this guide

The reader is encouraged to test the measurability of each goal by determining whether the required behavior is observable and whether the criterion clearly identifies the level of an acceptable performance.

(You may want to write your thoughts about the following down on a piece of scratch paper or enter them into your PC.)

Observable Behavior:

Specific Criterion:

R-ea-d-ing

1. Gobbledygook

Amber will improve ability to retell details or answer comprehension questions from reading at the fifth grade level by answering correctly with appropriate rationale 70% of the opportunities.

2. Discussion

According to the PLOPs on her IEP, (a) Amber wants "to try to read a lot more so I can understand what I read," (b) she "struggles in reading, writing, and vocabulary comprehension/use," (c) she needs to "see written material and make sense of it instead of working on phonetics and reading letter by letter," and (d) she "doesn't trust herself beyond one letter at a time so she doesn't try to say the whole word." Amber is a sophomore in high school, and "she plans to attend a junior college and then transfer to a four year college." The IEP team is "concerned not only with her decoding but also with (comprehension)." As a PLOP against which to judge the appropriateness of the goal, this information is of limited use. How well does Amber read? We really don't know, and we have no idea whether comprehending at a fifth grade level is an appropriate goal. So for the sake of goal-writing practice, we will assume it is appropriate. Is it measurable as written? Literally, it says that she will improve . . . by answering correctly 70% of the questions she is asked. Is that an adequate level of comprehension for any purpose? If her decoding is "letter-by-letter," doesn't that need serious attention so that her comprehension can be based on fluent, accurate decoding?

3. Goal

Given fifth grade material [we are assuming, skeptically, this level of difficulty is appropriate], Amber will orally read 100 words correct per minute and correctly answer 95% of the included comprehension questions.

4. Observable behavior:

(You may want to write your thoughts about the following down on a piece of scratch paper or enter them into your PC.)

Specific Criterion:

PLoPs Matter

1. Gobbledygook

Amber will demonstrate knowledge and use of the following language processes with 80% accuracy using literal and/or academic based material: noun identification, association, categorization, comparisons, descriptions and multiple-meaning words.

2. Discussion

When the excess verbiage is deleted from this purported "communication" goal, we are left with "demonstrate knowledge of noun identification, etc., with 80% accuracy." The only information in Amber's PLOP related to communication is that she "struggles with vocabulary comprehension/use," she would benefit from speech language services (90 minutes a month) and there is concern about "ordering thought process-sequencing." This GG is Amber's only goal other than her reading goal (our # 33). Does this GG address her communication needs, as best we can guess what they are? This GG illustrates, as does her preceding reading GG, that adequate PLOPs are an essential foundation for writing meaningful goals. If we don't know where we are now, how can we plot a course to where we want to be in a year?

While 80% accuracy in this context might be close to understandable (probably meaning 80% of items correct), the problem is the total lack of any information about the level of difficulty of the material that is to be the source for the knowledge demonstrations in all named areas. Obviously, such tasks using second grade materials would be different from the same tasks using 10th grade material. Since Amber's vocabulary (expressive and receptive) is an important issue, we will focus a goal on that.

3. Goal

Given fifty 10th grade vocabulary words selected from content texts, Amber will correctly use 45 or more of them correctly in sentences.

4. Observable behavior:

(You may want to write your thoughts down on a piece of scratch paper or enter them into your PC.)

Specific Criterion:

35 columbus

1. Gobbledygook (GG)

Tyler will navigate the world in school.

2. Discussion

Our final GG, like others we've seen, is lifted verbatim from a much lengthier general education state standard. In some states, IEP teams are required to locate a state standard that seems somehow connected to each goal. This probably stems from the popular misconception that the general curriculum needs to be in every IEP. In fact, the IEP is a special education document and should deal only with the individualized special education services and goals appropriate to help the student access the general curriculum. The attempt to derive an individualized goal from a general standard and/or to find a standard to cover an already properly developed goal is an unnecessary waste of time. Worse, linking all special education goals to the general education curriculum risks losing the essential individualization of the IEP and its services.

3. Goal

As to this particular standard-based GG, it is impossible to guess what the writer had in mind that Tyler should learn to do. Each reader is invited to write a goal for Tyler that has something to do with the world or with navigation. Tyler is a 15 year old who has a moderately severe learning disability.

4. Observable behavior:

(You may want to write your thoughts down on a piece of scratch paper or enter them into your PC.)

Specific Criterion:

On Your Own -- Having Fun

The next step is to practice converting four gobbledygooks into clean and neat annual measurable goals that would make any IEP proud.

Make any reasonable assumptions about Greg that are necessary. You also might want to look back at the seven tips in *Table 3 (page 19)*.

To get you started, a wee bit of guidance is provided

1. Gobbledygook

Greg will follow directions with 80% accuracy involving such actions as stop at the curb.

To Start

The observable behavior — follow directions — is fine. The 80% accuracy is nonsense. So a real criterion is needed. The GG writer seems to have been concerned with Greg following important directions, so ...

2. Gobbledygook

Greg will demonstrate the sequence of patterns 4 of 5 times.

To Start

We probably reproduce or copy, rather than demonstrate, a sequence. Does it matter whether the pattern is a picture of a cow followed by a horse versus seven abstract, geometric figures? Does it matter if the sequence is hidden after a few seconds or stays in view?

3. Gobbledygook

Greg will develop life skills, stress management and coping skills.

To Start

The good news is that a huge variety of measurable goals could have been behind this GG. This is also the bad news. From the first two GGs above, written for Greg, one can assume he performs at a fairly low level — probably below a 4-year old level. So, a good possibility would be to think about a self-help (life) skill he probably needs to acquire ...

4. Gobbledygook

Greg will increase motor skills and participate in various activities 70% of the time.

To Start

This GG is pretty awful, but we can tell the direction the GG was headed. Maybe the behavior could be something like, "Greg participates in motor activities?" And the criterion ...

Finally, Good News

In the last five years the elementary education world has begun to respond to the new federal law mandate that public schools use scientifically-based instruction (especially in reading) and objectively and frequently monitor children's progress. The hope and belief is that better instruction and monitoring will reduce the numbers of children who qualify for special education services, including IEPs.

Curriculum-based assessment, using fluency (speed and accuracy) data, is rapidly gaining widespread acceptance. Among the many benefits of assessing children's academic status by using fluency data is that the writing of present levels of performance and goals is hugely simplified. Furthermore, PLOPs and goals based on fluency are legally impeccable and educationally meaningful, practical and easy to understand. The process of curriculum-based assessment, using fluency data, is very efficient, requiring only a fraction of the time of other assessments and producing more readily usable information.

More than 90 years ago, Starch (1915) collected oral reading fluency data from over 3,500 students in Wisconsin, Minnesota and New York. In spring of 2005, Hasbrouck and Tindal collected similar data for several thousand students in several districts. The comparison is seen in *Table 4* (page 103).

Oral Reading Fluency

Table 4

	Grade 1	Grade 2	Grade 3	Grade 4	Grade 5	Grade 6	Grade 7	Grade 8
1915[1]	90[a]	108	126	144	168	192	216	240
2005[2]	59	89	107	125	138	150	150	151

[a] Words Per Minute

[1] Starch, D. (1915). The measurement of efficiency in reading. *The Journal of Educational Psychology*, 6(1), 1-24.
[2] Behavioral Research and Teaching (2005). *Oral Reading Fluency: 90 years of Research*. Eugene, OR: University of Oregon. http://brt.uoregon.edu

The decline in oral reading fluency over the years is marked. As the use of rate data becomes more common, and more instructional attention is given to fluency, we may expect to see improvement at all grade levels. Many believe we should distinguish between data such as that shown in *Table 4*, which is normative, i.e., it describes what students actually do, from standards, which represent a desired performance. Most Response-to-Intervention (RTI) models now being advocated suggest using such normative norms (local, state or national) for determining whether a performance is proficient and for goal setting. This kind of data can be collected readily for any observable and countable behavior, whether it be academic, social or other.

As time goes by, rate and fluency data will become ever more widely used. Local districts, buildings, and grade levels will collect the data and have their own norms. It will be easier and easier to find and observe programs that are using this system for assessing PLOPs and writing goals. Soon there may be no Gobbledygooks, only clear and measurable goals, written accurately and easily and perhaps even with a dash of pleasure.